HORIZONS

Reading to Learn

Fast Track C–D
Literature Anthology

Siegfried Engelmann

Susan Hanner

SRA
McGraw-Hill

Columbus, Ohio

A Division of The McGraw-Hill Companies

ACKNOWLEDGMENTS

*Grateful acknowledgment is made to the following authors, agents,
and publishers for permissions to use copyrighted materials:*

Annick Press Ltd.
STEPHANIE'S PONYTAIL by Robert Munsch. Copyright © 1996 by Robert Munsch.
Reprinted by permission of Annick Press Ltd.

Farrar, Straus & Giroux, Inc.
THE THREE WISHES by Margot Zemach. Text and illustrations
by Margot Zemach. Copyright © 1986 by Margot Zemach. Reprinted
by permission of Farrar, Straus & Giroux, Inc.

HarperCollins Publishers
AMELIA BEDELIA by Peggy Parish. Text copyright © 1963
by Margaret Parish. Used by permission of HarperCollins Publishers.

THE SOUP STONE by Maria Leach. Copyright © 1954
by Funk & Wagnalls Co. Used by permission of HarperCollins Publishers.

McGraw-Hill Companies
WON-LDY PAYE. "Why Leopard Has Black Spots". Copyright © 1991
by Won-Ldy Paye. Used by permission of the McGraw-Hill Companies.

Melissa Heckler
"A House with a Star Inside." Copyright © 1991
by Melissa Heckler. Used with permission of the author.

Simon & Schuster
"Boar Out There" from EVERY LIVING THING
by Cynthia Rylant. Copyright © 1985 Cynthia Rylant. Reprinted with
the permission of Simon & Schuster Books for Young Readers, an
imprint of Simon & Schuster Children's Publishing Division.

SRA/McGraw-Hill

*A Division of The **McGraw·Hill** Companies*

TABLE OF CONTENTS

TABLE OF CONTENTS
(cont'd)

Stephanie's Ponytail

Story by Robert Munsch
Art by Michael Martchenko

One day Stephanie went to her mom and said, "None of the kids in my class have a ponytail. I want a nice ponytail coming right out the back."

So Stephanie's mom gave her a nice ponytail coming right out the back.

When Stephanie went to school the other kids looked at her and said, "Ugly, ugly, *very* ugly."

Stephanie said, "It's *my ponytail* and *I* like it."

The next morning, when Stephanie went to school, all the other girls had ponytails coming out the back.

Stephanie looked at them and said, "You are all a bunch of copycats. You just do whatever I do. You don't have a brain in your heads."

5

The next morning the mom said, "Stephanie, would you like a ponytail coming out the back?"

Stephanie said, "No."

"Then that's that," said her mom. "That's the only place you can do ponytails."

"No, it's not," said Stephanie. "I want one coming out the side, just above my ear."

"Very strange," said the mom. "Are you sure that is what you want?"

"Yes," said Stephanie.

So her mom gave Stephanie a nice ponytail coming out right above her ear.

When she went to school the other kids saw her and said, "Ugly, ugly, *very* ugly."

Stephanie said, "It's *my ponytail* and *I* like it."

The next morning when Stephanie came to school all the girls, and even some of the boys, had nice ponytails coming out just above their ears.

The next morning the mom said, "Stephanie, would you like a ponytail coming out the back?"

Stephanie said, "NNNO."

"Would you like one coming out the side?"

"NNNO!"

"Then that's that," said her mom. "There is no other place you can do ponytails."

"Yes, there is," said Stephanie. "I want one coming out the top of my head like a tree."

"That's very, very strange," said her mom. "Are you sure that is what you want?"

"Yes," said Stephanie.

So her mom gave Stephanie a nice
ponytail coming out the top of her head
like a tree. When Stephanie went to
school, the other kids saw her and said,
"Ugly, ugly, *very* ugly."

Stephanie said, "It's *my ponytail* and
I like it."

The next day all of the girls
and all of the boys had
ponytails coming out
the top. It looked
like broccoli was
growing out of
their heads.

The next morning the mom said, "Stephanie, would you like a ponytail coming out the back?"

Stephanie said, "NNNO."

"Would you like one coming out the side?"

"NNNO!"

"Would you like one coming out the top?"

"NNNO!"

"Then that is definitely that," said the mom. "There is no other place you can do ponytails."

"Yes, there is," said Stephanie. "I want one coming out the front and hanging down in front of my nose."

"But nobody will know if you are coming or going," her mom said. "Are you sure that is what you want?"

"Yes," said Stephanie. So her mom gave Stephanie a nice ponytail coming out the front.

On the way to school she bumped into four trees, three cars, two houses and one Principal. When she finally got to her class the other kids saw her and said, "Ugly, ugly, *very* ugly." Stephanie said, "It's *my ponytail* and *I* like it."

15

The next day all of the girls and all of the boys, and even the teacher, had ponytails coming out the front and hanging down in front of their noses. None of them could see where they were going. They bumped into the desks and they bumped into each other. They bumped into the walls, and, by mistake, three girls went into the boys' bathroom.

Stephanie yelled, "You are a bunch of brainless copycats. You just do whatever I do. When I come tomorrow I am going to have. . . SHAVED MY HEAD!"

The first person to come the next day was the teacher. She had shaved her head and she was bald.

The next to come were the boys. They had shaved their heads and they were bald.

The next to come were the girls. They had shaved their heads and they were bald.

The last person to come was Stephanie, and she had. . .

a nice little ponytail coming right out the back.

21

GEORGE AT THE ZOO

Written by Sally George
Illustrated by Rob Mancini

George was a small dog who liked large bones and going on picnics. So when his family got out the picnic basket, George got very excited.

"No, George!" said his family. "We're going to the zoo. Dogs can't go to the zoo."

But George liked going in the car, and
smelling new smells, and running in new
places, and, especially, eating the picnic.
So when his family wasn't looking,
George jumped inside the picnic basket.
The lid closed, and nobody saw him.

They picked up the picnic basket and
carried it out to the car. It was very dark in
the picnic basket. And very crowded.

There was more room after George ate the
cold chicken, and the ham, and the rolls, and
half the cake.

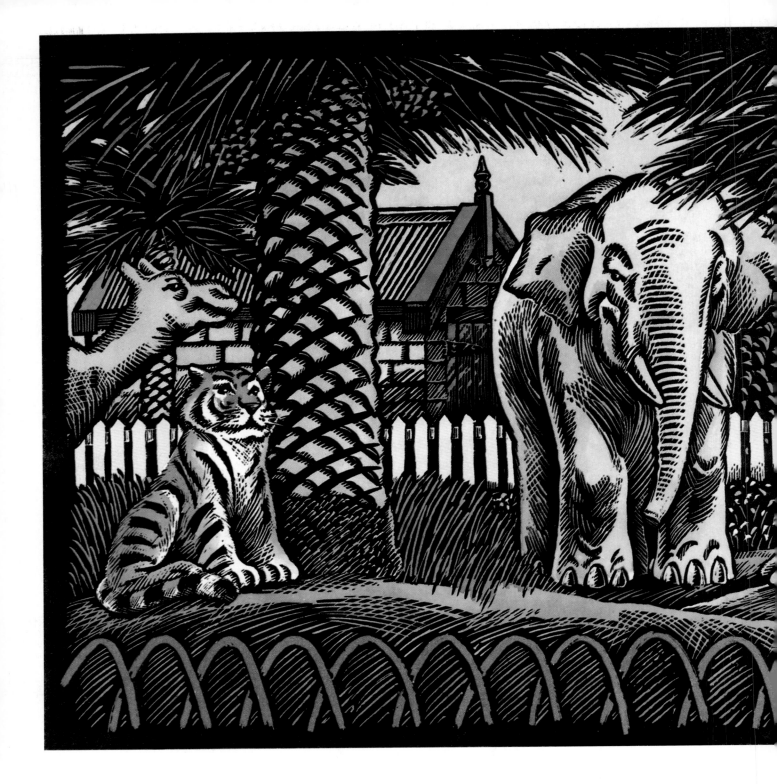

George's family went into the zoo. "This is
a very heavy picnic basket," they said. But
they didn't open it. George pushed his nose
through the lid.

He smelled lions and tigers, and elephants
and camels, and bears and giraffes, and emus
and ostriches.

George liked the zoo.

His family walked and walked all over the zoo. Finally, they sat down. They opened the picnic basket.

"Oh, George!" they said. "Bad dog, George!"

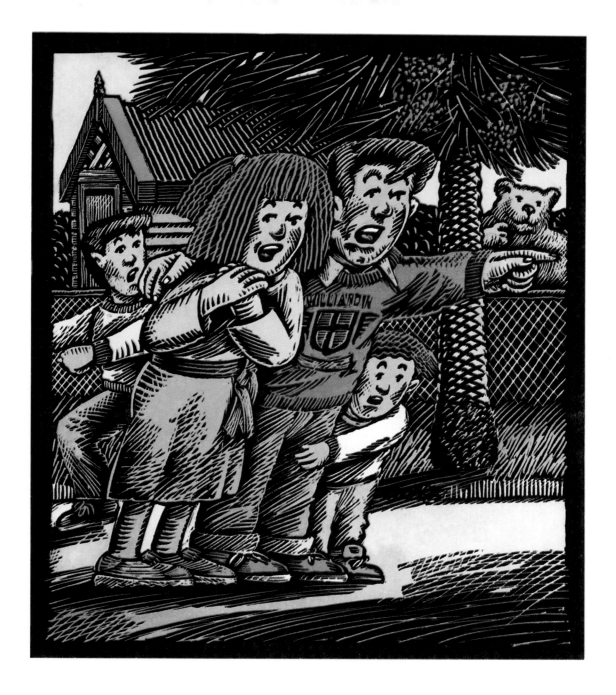

They were just about to shut the lid,
when—men began to shout, women began
to scream, and the children began to run.

George jumped out of the picnic basket.
There was the biggest cat he had ever seen.
And the cat had the biggest bone he had
ever seen.

George forgot that he had just eaten the cold chicken, and the ham, and the rolls, and half the cake.

George wanted that bone!

George's family sat in a tree and called him. But George wanted that bone.

He growled and barked and snapped at the cat. The cat came closer, and roared back the biggest growl that George had ever heard.

George growled and barked and snapped again. The cat stopped, and men came running with trucks and ropes and nets, and chased it into a big cage.

The men locked the cage with a big lock. The men and the women and the children stopped screaming. Everyone looked at George.

George did not want to be chased with
trucks and ropes and nets and be locked in
a big cage.

He ran back to his picnic basket.

George's family got out of the tree. He
knew that they would say, "Bad dog, George!"
    But they didn't. They seemed quite happy.
They said he was a good dog, a wonderful
dog, the bravest, best lion-chasing dog in the
whole world.

Then they picked up the picnic basket
and carried it past the sign that said,
"No Dogs Allowed," and back to the car.

And when they got home, George took
the lion's bone out of the picnic basket . . .
and buried it in the garden.

POP'S TRUCK

Written by Honey Andersen and Bill Reinholtd
Illustrated by Pam Posey

Dan and Wendy liked going to Pop's
house because he lived on a farm.
There were sheep, chickens,
pigs, one cow, and an
old dog to play with at
Pop's farm.
But best of all, there
was Pop's truck.
"Your truck is great,
Pop," Dan always said.

Pop let the children ride in the back of the
truck when he fed out hay to the sheep
and the cow.

He let them ride in the back of
the truck when he went to check
the fences.

Once, he let Wendy sit in the
back holding a lamb when its
mother was sick.

Pop had to bring the ewe and
her lamb up to the sheds, to
look after them.

Dan had to sit on the ewe
to keep her still, while Pop's
truck bounced over the dirt
road all the way home.

45

But last week, when Wendy and Dan went out to stay at Pop's, they found that something was wrong.

"Hi, Pop! Where's the truck?" asked Dan.

"Oh, Dan, it's a long, sad story," replied Pop. "That truck has been on the farm as long as Granny and I have. It's as old as your mom."

"It's a great truck, Pop," said Dan.

46

"It *was* a great truck, Dan, but it's had a long life. Last week, it just seemed to get too tired to go any more."

"It probably needs a new battery or something," Dan said.

"Take it to the garage and get Jim to fix it," Wendy suggested.

"I tried that. The trouble is, it's so old that Jim can't get parts to fix it."

"Well, where is it, anyway?" asked Dan.

"It's been taken to the dump."

"What?" yelled Wendy.

"You can't take the truck to the dump. It's part of the family," said Dan. "How would you like to be taken to the dump just because you'd got old and tired?"

"Well, that's where it is," said Pop. "I can't have useless machinery lying around the farm. Come and look at the new truck I bought. It's in the garage."

"I don't even want to see it," said Wendy. "I'd rather go to the dump and see the old truck."

"Yes, so would I," agreed Dan.

"Well, how about a ride in the back of the new truck, down to the dump? You could say good-bye to the old one," suggested Pop.

"O.K."

Wendy and Dan ran to the garage, and there was a very shiny, new blue truck.

"The old truck never had to go in the garage," muttered Dan. "It was tough enough to live outside for thirty years."

"I hate blue trucks," Wendy said to Dan, as she scrambled into the back of the new truck. "And there are no old sacks in the back to sit on."

They sat quietly in the back of the truck,
while Pop drove down the driveway to the gate.
Dan hopped out, opened the gate, and then
closed it after Pop had driven through.

As they drove down the road to the dump,
they noticed that the new truck wasn't
nearly as bumpy to ride in.

"I can't even see the old truck," said Wendy. "Can you, Dan?"

"No. Oh . . . Oh, yes, I mean. Look, Wendy! There it is. It's just over there, by the storage shed. But why is it up there, instead of down in the valley with all the junk?"

The old truck was parked on the top of the hill, with its cab and engine pointing down into the dump. It seemed to be looking over the whole scene.

As Pop stopped near the old truck, the children were surprised to see that someone was sitting in the front.

It was Dave, the man in charge of the dump. He was having a cup of tea, and he had his thermos propped up on the seat next to his paper.

"Hello, Bill," he said to Pop. "That truck of yours was just too good to bury with all the garbage. I got the boys to haul it up here for me. It makes a great office. It keeps me warm and dry. It's a great truck."

"There you are, Pop," whispered Dan. "Why didn't you think of that? You could have used it for an office at the farm."

"Well, Dan, you're probably right," replied Pop. "But to tell you the truth, I don't really need an office that badly."

54

"Well, at least someone can still use it," said Dan. "And it didn't have to be crushed to pieces."

"And," Wendy said to Dave, "you get a really good view from here!"

55

"What about coming into my office for
a cup of tea?" asked Dave.
"That would be great," said Wendy.
"That would be terrific," said Dan.

Trixie

Written by Rick Brownell

Illustrated by Joy Antonie

I love going to the
dump. There's always
so much to see. The
seagulls must think so,
too, because there are
always millions of them
flying around.

I remember the day I first saw
Trixie. Dad and I had just arrived at
the dump and we were starting to unload
the station wagon. A dog walked up to the car.

"Look, Dad!" I said. "That dog has only
three legs."

"Well, it sure does. Poor thing must have been
hit by a car. It probably had to have that leg taken
off by the vet."

"Dad, can I pet her?"

Dad took a closer look at
the three-legged dog and said,
"Come here, Girl." He clicked his
tongue a couple of times and the
three-legged dog came up to him. She
seemed a little shy, but her tail was wagging.
Dad put his hand out and let the dog sniff it
so she would know he wanted to be friendly.
Then he petted her on the head.

"She seems to be friendly. I think it's O.K.
for you to pet her," he said.

As soon as I put out
my hand, the three-legged
dog gave it a big lick. I
think she liked me right
away. I sure liked her!

"Dad, I like this dog and she likes
me. Can I take her home?"

Just as Dad was about to answer,
there was a loud whistle.

"Get over here, Trixie, and stop
bothering those people."

As the man walked
toward us, I said, "This
dog's not bothering us,
Mister. She's a nice
dog. Is she yours?"

"Oh, yes. She's mine all right.
I've had Trixie since she was a pup. Of
course, with one leg missing, she doesn't
get around as well as she used to, but she
does all right."

Dad finished dumping the trash and said,
"Come on, Emma. It's time to go."

"Goodbye, Trixie. See you next time."

From then on,
seeing Trixie was
the best part of
going to the dump.
We discovered that
Gus, Trixie's owner,
worked at the dump and that Trixie
went to work with Gus every day.

I'd always look for Trixie as we pulled into the
dump. I'd jump out of the car as Trixie headed
our way. I knew she was happy to see me
because her tail would be wagging—but not so
hard that it would make her fall down.

I'd give Trixie a big
pet and scratch her above
the tail the way she liked it.
Then I'd throw a stick for her to
fetch while Dad unloaded the car. Trixie
was a good fetcher, but I never threw the
stick too far, because Gus had told me that I
shouldn't make Trixie too tired.

    One day, as Gus
wandered over, he said,
"Hi, Emma. I see you're
watching my dog for me again."

    "Hello, Gus," I said. "Yes, I'm
taking good care of her. I'm not
throwing the stick too far, though. Gus,
how did Trixie lose her leg?"

    "Well, Emma," Gus said, "Trixie always liked
to run out in the woods to chase the squirrels
and just wander around. Once, she didn't show
up after dark, and I began to worry.

"The next morning, I went out to look for her. I searched all day long and finally found her, caught in a trap.

"She'd been lying there all night and was so weak that she couldn't even lift her head. So I put her over my shoulders and carried her home.

"That trap had hurt
her leg pretty badly,
and it was easy to see
that she was in pain.
The vet thought it
would be best to just put
her to sleep. But I couldn't stand the
thought of losing Trixie. She's my best friend.
The vet said that the only way she might live
would be to take her wounded leg off."

"That must have been awful for you, Gus, and
for Trixie," I said.

"Yes, Emma. It was. After the operation she was
a pretty sick pooch. I didn't know if she would ever
be well enough to get up out of her bed.

"Then one day,
I was sitting at
the kitchen table,
and I heard a clippity,
clippity, clop sound. I turned
around and there was Trixie standing
on her three legs, wagging her tail."

"She's really a great dog, Gus."

"Yes. She's my best friend, aren't you,
Trixie?" Gus said, as he petted her.

Several weeks later,
Dad and I took another
load of junk to the dump.
As usual, I looked for Trixie,
but she didn't come running up to the car.

"Do you see her, Dad?" I asked.

"No, I don't, Emma. But don't worry, she'll
show up. She always does," Dad said. "Come
on. Help me unload the car."

I kept a look out for
Trixie as I helped unload the car.

"Dad, I can't even see Gus."

"Perhaps Gus and Trixie have
the day off," Dad said. I knew he was
worried, too.

"Perhaps Gus doesn't work here any
more. But we'll drive around to the other
side in case he's working over there."

And there he was—coming out of a shed.
I jumped out of the car and ran up to Gus.

"Gus, where have you been? We've been looking all over for you."

"Well, hello, Emma," Gus said. "I've been kind of busy. You see, I've been playing nurse for Trixie."

"For Trixie? Is she O.K.?" I exclaimed.

"Come and see for yourself," Gus said.

Dad and I followed Gus to the shed. It was dark, so it took a minute before we could see.

"It must have happened early this morning," Gus said, as he pointed to the corner.

And there lay
Trixie—with six little
golden puppies cuddled
up to her.

"Oh, Trixie!" I exclaimed.
Trixie's tail started wagging
as she heard my voice. "Oh, your
babies—they're just beautiful!"

"They sure are!" said Gus. "But in two
months I'm going to have six more dogs than
I know what to do with."

He looked at Dad and then at me and then
back at Dad.

"I wonder how I'm going to find homes for them.
Any ideas about a home for one?" he said, as he
winked at Dad.

"Dad! Gus! I know
someone who needs a
puppy. *I* need one. Really I do!"
Dad looked down at me with
a smile and said, "I'm sure you do.
And why not!"
I'm sure Trixie smiled before she shut
her eyes and went to sleep.
And I'm sure one puppy smiled, too. She's
going to be my puppy soon.

THE THREE WISHES

• An Old Story •

Written and illustrated by Margot Zemach

Long ago, a man and his wife lived peacefully at the edge of a great forest. All the year round, they worked together as woodcutters.

Every morning, at sunrise, they went into the forest, where they cut trees and branches into logs. At sunset, they carried them home. But no matter how hard or how long they worked, they often went hungry.

Early one morning, as they were working in the forest, they heard a faint voice calling: "Help, help, someone help me!" The voice seemed to be coming from an old tree that had fallen nearby.

The man and his wife ran to the tree. There on the ground lay a small imp kicking his legs. His tail was caught under the fallen tree! "Help, Help," the imp cried weakly.

"We'll help you gladly," the man and his wife said together. And they pushed and pushed till the tree rolled off.

The imp sprang straight up into the air, joyfully twirling his tail. "A hundred thanks for your kindness," he said. "I have been lying here in misery ever since this tree fell. To thank you for saving me, I will give you three wishes. There are only three, so wish wisely, my friends—and goodbye!" Then he flew up among the branches and disappeared.

The man and his wife were delighted with their good luck. All that cold day, they were warmed by thoughts of the three wishes that would soon be theirs. "We might wish for fine clothes and silver," thought the wife, "or even for a grand house with flower gardens and fruit trees."

In the evening, as they trudged home, the man thought: "We might wish for a donkey to carry this wood, or even a horse and cart to ride in."

"That's so, that's so," he said to himself, and his bundle of wood seemed to grow lighter.

When they got home, the man and his wife settled down to talk about their three wishes. "We might wish for fine clothes and silver," said the wife, "or a grand house with beautiful flower gardens and fruit trees."

"Or we might wish for a donkey to carry the wood, or even a horse and cart to ride in ourselves," said the man.

"Or we might wish for great chests of jewels," said the wife.

"Or even a mountain of gold coins!" said the man.

"We might wish never to go hungry again," said the wife.

"That's so, that's so," said the man. "But just now I wish we had a pan of sausages for our dinner."

No sooner said than done. That very instant, a pan of sausages appeared, sizzling and smoking on the fire.

"Oh, you fool!" cried the wife. "Look what you've done! How I wish those sausages were hanging from your big nose!"

No sooner said than done. The sausages leaped from the pan and hung heavily from the man's nose.

"Oh, wife, see what you've done!" he cried. "Who's the fool now?"

The man and his wife tried every which way to get the sausages off. But, pull and tug as they might, all their efforts were useless. The sausages remained hanging from the poor man's nose.

Finally, too tired to move, the man and his wife slumped down before the fire.

They thought with longing of their one last wish. Should it be the donkey to carry the wood, the horse and cart to ride in together, the grand house, the fine clothes and jewels, or the mountain of gold coins? Any one of these wishes could still be theirs.

But what would be the good of it if the man must live his whole life with sausages hanging from his nose?

So they joined hands, and with their last wish they wished the sausages OFF.

No sooner said than done! The sausages were back in the pan, sizzling and smoking and smelling delicious.

So the man and his wife sat down cheerfully to a fine dinner.

"Well now, we've not done too badly," said the wife.

"That's so, that's so!" the man agreed.

A House with a Star Inside

A story retold by Melissa Heckler
Illustrated by Holly Hannon

Once upon a time there was a little boy. Oh, he was maybe six or seven years old. One day he went to his mother and he said, "I'm bored." His mother looked at him and he looked at her, and she said with a twinkle in her eye, "You go outside and see if you can find me a little red, round house with no windows and no doors, a chimney on top, and a star inside."

The boy thought about that. Houses weren't round. A round, red house with no windows, no doors, a chimney on top, and a star inside?

Well, he was out the door quickly. He looked around his neighborhood, but all he saw were square houses and houses with windows and doors. He saw lots of chimneys, but he saw no stars, at least not from the outside, so he went on down the road. He was walking and walking, and he saw a girl. He said to her, "Have you seen a red, round house with no windows, no doors, a chimney on top, and a star inside?"

The girl thought for a minute and then she said, "No, I haven't seen a house like that anywhere. I've seen square houses, and I've seen long houses, and I've seen thin houses, but I've never seen a red, round house. But, you know, my father's a farmer, and maybe he'll know 'cause he's seen lots of things."

So the girl and the boy walked on back to her
father's farm, and they walked on into the barn where
her father was standing. He paused when he saw the
two children. They went right up to him and the little
girl said, "Papa, this little boy needs some help."

The boy asked the farmer, "Have you seen a red,
round house with no windows, no doors, a chimney.
on top, and a star inside?"

The farmer said, "Hmmmm. I've seen red barns. I've
seen all kinds of differently shaped houses. In fact, I've
even seen round barns, but I've never seen a red,
round house with no windows, no doors, a chimney
on top, and a star inside. But I have an idea. You go
on down the road and ask Granny. Granny's likely to
be sitting out on her front porch rocking. She's old
and she's seen lots of things in her time. Maybe she'll
have seen one."

So the boy thanked the farmer and the girl, and he ran on down the road till he came to Granny's house. He opened the gate and he went up the front steps. He stopped right on Granny's front porch. "Granny!" he said.

"Good morning," said Granny. "Good morning," said the boy. "Granny, Granny, I'm looking for a red, round house with no windows, no doors, a chimney on top, and a star inside. Have you ever seen one like that?"

Granny rocked and rocked and rocked, then she said, "I've seen lots of things in my day. I've seen lots of kinds of houses, but I've never seen a red, round house with no windows, no doors, a chimney on top, and a star inside. But I'd sure like to read of an evening in a house with a star inside, so if you find that house, you come back and tell me." Granny rocked some more. "Now I have an idea," she said. "You go out into the road and you go ask the wind, because the wind has seen everything and been everywhere. I think perhaps the wind will tell you."

91

So the boy thanked Granny. He ran down the steps, ran back out the gate, and he just stood in the middle of the road. He opened his arms wide and he shouted, "WIND! WIND! HAVE YOU SEEN A RED, ROUND HOUSE WITH NO WINDOWS, NO DOORS, A CHIMNEY ON TOP, AND A STAR INSIDE?"

Then he waited. Pretty soon he felt a little push at his back. Just a little breeze, it was. But as he waited, the breeze picked up. It was just a little wind, but it seemed to be pushing the boy down the road. So he just went on, feeling the wind at his back, and it pushed him right up a hill. When he got to the top of that hill, the wind pushed him just a little farther, until he was standing right beneath a tree. He looked up at the tree. He saw its leaves.

Through the leaves he saw one other thing. It was
an apple. Just then, the wind came, and it blew that
apple right off the tree so it fell down at the boy's
feet. The boy picked up the apple, and he looked at it.
It was red and round. It had no windows, no door,
and a chimney on top. But where was the star?

The boy didn't wait more than ten seconds. He ran
off down the road. He ran past Granny's house and
he yelled, "Granny, I think I've found it. I'll come back
and show you!"

He ran on to his mother. He ran through the front
door of his house and he called, "Mama! Mama! I
think I've found it!"

His mother came. When she saw he had an apple, she got out a knife and sat down at the kitchen table. She lay the apple on its side and carefully cut it in half. There, right in the center of each half, was a beautiful five-pointed star!

Well, the boy did go back to Granny, and he went back to the farmer and to the girl, too. He showed them all what he had found: a red, round house with no windows, no doors, a chimney on top, and a star inside.

Tom's Friend

Written and Illustrated
by Pat Reynolds

"Mom! Where are you? Look what I've found!"
Tom came running up to the back door, excited
and out of breath.

"He was by the long grass near the back fence.
Probably lives in the bushes along the creek. He
likes me, Mom. Look. you can tell—he's smiling.
And he didn't run away. I was very gentle with
him. He didn't mind when I picked him up. He
likes me and I want to keep him . . ."

"What have you got there?" asked his mom.

Tom held out the bucket she used to water her plants.

Curled up in the bottom was a big lizard. It didn't fit in the bucket very well, and it looked up at them awkwardly with one bright eye.

"Look at his nose holes," said Tom. He pointed to the bucket, but his hand shot back again when the lizard threw open its mouth and revealed a very blue tongue.

"Why did he do that?" Tom was shocked that his new friend had been unfriendly.

"You frightened him, so he tried to scare you off. That's how he protects himself from dogs and cats and big birds."

"Well it's a good trick!" said Tom.

"He must be a bluetongue lizard. I think I'll call him Bluey. He can be my new pet. I'm going to make him a home right now. This bucket is too small." And he rushed off.

"Wait a minute . . ." called Mom.

But Tom didn't hear her, and she went inside with a half-smile, half-frown on her face.

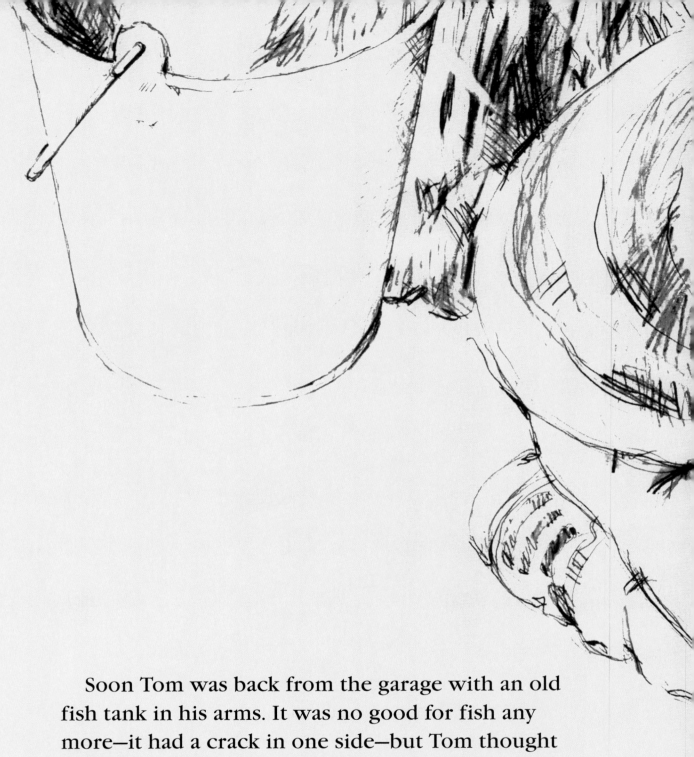

Soon Tom was back from the garage with an old
fish tank in his arms. It was no good for fish any
more—it had a crack in one side—but Tom thought
it might be comfortable for a lizard.

He filled the bottom with sand and rocks. Then
he put a dish in one corner, for water, and planted
some tufts of grass in the other.

"It's ready, Mom," he called.

He put on one of her gardening gloves, just
to be safe, and gently carried the lizard from
the bucket to the glass tank.

"There you go, Bluey," he murmured.

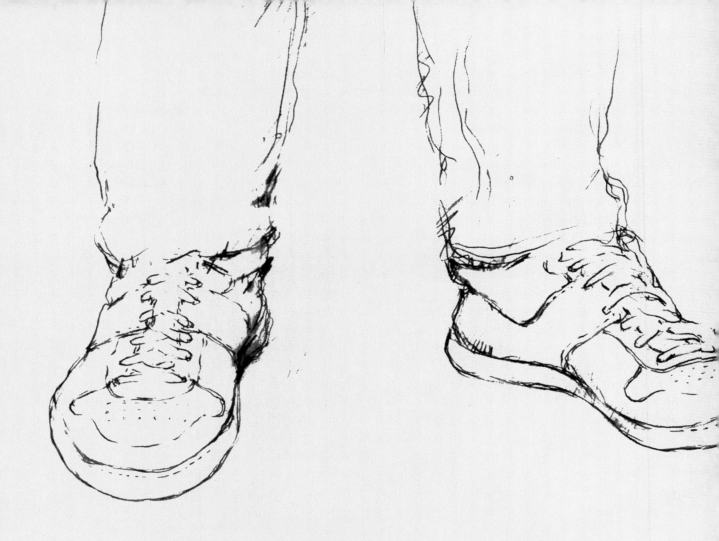

Mom came out to have a look. Tom certainly tried hard to make a good home for the lizard.

"See," he said, very pleased with himself. "He can move around now. He has water to drink, and somewhere to hide under that grass. What do lizards eat, Mom? Insects and things like that?"

"Yes, I think so. And fruit."

"Do you think he would eat hamburger?"
"Probably."
But there was something wrong. Mom
didn't look happy.
"Did I forget something?" Tom asked.

"Well, yes and no," said Mom with that
half-smile, half-frown.

Tom protested. "He has everything he
needs. What have I forgotten?"

"Come with me, Tom."

She held his hand and they walked down
to the bottom of the backyard.

"Show me where you found the lizard."

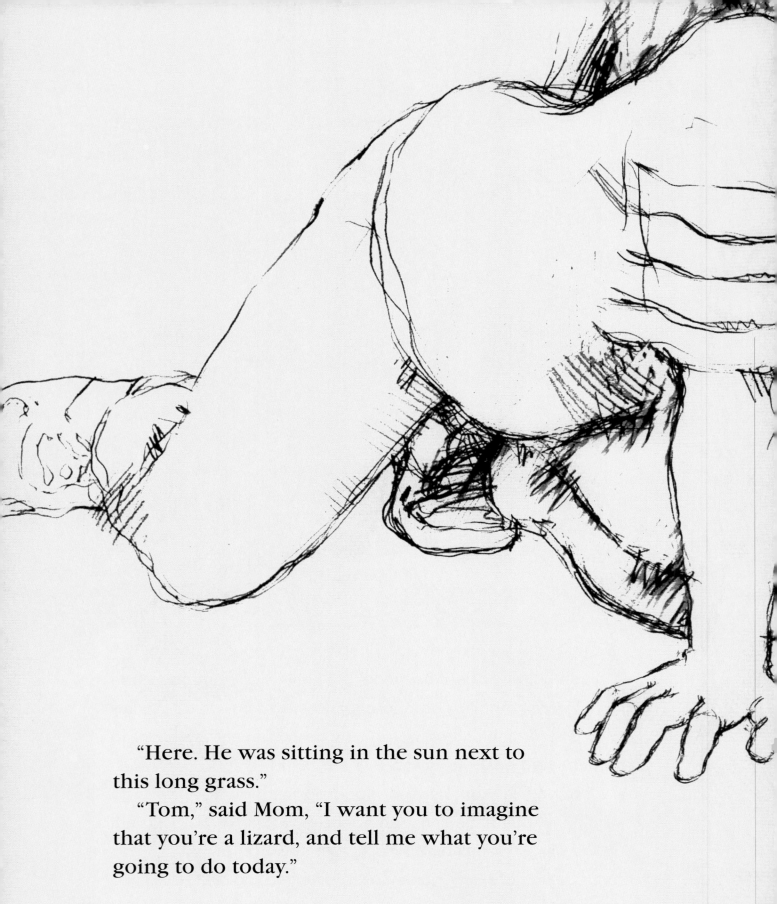

"Here. He was sitting in the sun next to this long grass."

"Tom," said Mom, "I want you to imagine that you're a lizard, and tell me what you're going to do today."

Tom's eyes lit up. "O.K.," he said. "Well, first I'm going to lie in the sun here for awhile. Then I'll creep down there, through the long grass, to the creek for a drink. Then . . . I think I'll catch some fat ants for lunch, over there where they live in that mound. And now I'll stretch out on that big flat rock over there, by the water, and have my after-lunch nap."

"I might go for a walk up the creek after that, to see what's there, since you never let me go that far, and then . . ."

"Let's go back to the house now," said Mom. And they walked back, with Tom pulling her up the hill because she always pretended to be out of breath.

"Can you see what's missing now?"

Tom looked at the lizard in the tank and his face grew sad. He knew what she meant.

"I think I'd better let him go, Mom," he said.

Mom squeezed his hand. "I think Bluey really likes you for that. Look, he's smiling!"

See the Rabbits

Written by Harvey Cleaver
Illustrated by Ted Tadiello

One day a few years ago, when I was six years old, my parents told me, "This weekend, we're going to see the rabbits in Iowa."

I was standing next to my older brother Gordey. We had just come home from school.

Gordey said, "Isn't that where Aunt Jen and Uncle Dick live?"

"That's right," Dad said. "Do you remember the last time we went there?"

"Sure," Gordey said. "It was just after we got the blue Ford. I remember it broke down when we were in Iowa, and we spent a whole day in the garage, waiting for it to get fixed."

"Yes," Mom said. "That part of the visit was not too much fun." Then Mom turned to me and asked, "Do you remember the trip, Dennis?"

"I . . . I . . ." I didn't remember one thing. I'd heard the names Dick and Jen, but I didn't have memories of any faces to go with the names.

"Well," Dad said to me, "you were less than three years old the last time we visited them. So you probably had other things to think about."

Gordey said, "Either that or he forgot to wind up his mind that weekend."

"Not funny," I said to Gordey and made my best sour face at him, but he was already making his goofy face at me and saying, "Gee, I don't remember anything. I was just a little baby."

"Well, I can't help it," I said.

It was Wednesday and we were going to leave on Saturday morning, very early. That meant I had to get ready for a long car trip. I always had two kinds of problems on these trips. The first problem was trying to sit in a car hour after hour without going nuts. The other problem was Gordey. He would always do something to get me mad. Then we'd argue until Mom and Dad would make us stop.

This time, it would be different. I'd bring along all kinds of things so I wouldn't get bored—paper, crayons, books, games. And then if Mom and Dad would just let me sit in the front seat by the window, Gordey wouldn't be able to start anything.

Before we left on the trip, Dad took out a map and showed everybody the road we would take. Dad touched the town where we lived in Illinois and said, "We're going to take this road to Iowa, and all the way to see the rabbits." He traced a red line with his finger. When he stopped, he said, "It's going to take us more than five hours, so Gordey and Dennis, I want you to relax and be patient."

I wanted to be patient, but I didn't know how long five hours felt.

Even before we left, I was getting impatient. After we were already sitting in the car with all our stuff, Mom said that we had to go to the bathroom before we left. I told her that I didn't have to go, but she insisted.

I didn't get to sit in the front seat by the window. Mom did. I could have sat in the middle of the front seat, but that's the worst seat in the whole car. You don't even have your own window. So I sat in the back with you-know-who. Before we were a block from home, he started to mess with the paper I had brought along. "That's mine," I explained. "If you want paper, bring your own."

"Now, now," Mom said. "There's enough paper for both of you. I'm sure you won't mind sharing with your brother." Mind? I hated it.

"Why can't he bring his own things?" I asked. "Why does he always have to . . ."

"Settle down," Dad said.

Just then, I saw two kids that we played with—Eddie and Amy. I rolled my window down, waved at them, and announced, "We're on our way to see the rabbits in Iowa." I had to talk very fast because we were moving at 30 miles an hour.

Mom thought it would be fun to play license-plate games. So first we played a color game. You'd get a point if you saw a red license plate. The Illinois plates were white, and that's what most of the cars had. The game was boring because we went for a long time before anybody spotted a red plate. Then guess who saw three of them and won the game? Gordey. I saw only one.

So we played another license-plate game. Dad said, "Let's see who gets the most license plates that start with the number nine." That was more fun than the red game. Mom won this game. I came in last, of course.

Then we played the out-of-state license game. You'd get a point for every out-of-state plate you spotted. Mom and Gordey tied in this game. By now, I was really tired of license-plate games. So I decided to draw some pictures. Mom said, "Why don't you draw a picture of the family?"

That was a good idea. I had drawn a large picture of the family in school, and everybody there thought it was great. I was working with smaller paper than I had in school, but I was being very careful. When I was done, my picture had a nice blue sky on top and green grass along the bottom. Dad and Mom were in the middle. I was next to Dad. Gordey was next to Mom.

I was wearing my big hiking boots and my thick belt. Dad was wearing a big cowboy hat. Everybody in the family had their arms out to the side, and we were smiling. Gordey's smile looked a little funny. I think the car went over some bumps when I was drawing him. So his lips were big and sort of crooked.

I told everybody, "I'm done."

"Let's see," Mom said. I handed her the picture. "Very nice," she said. "I see that you're wearing your new hiking boots."

Dad said to her, "Oh, is that supposed to be Dennis? He's bigger than Gordey."

"Let me see that picture," Gordey said. Mom held it up, and Gordey started to go on and on about what a bad picture it was. He laughed, "Hee haw, hee haw." Then he said, "So that little thing on the end is supposed to be me? I'm glad you didn't draw the dog in this picture because she probably would have been bigger than me, too. What a terrible looking picture."

"It's a nice picture," Mom said. "It's not that easy to draw things the size you want."

"Sure," Gordey said as he looked right at me. "I can't draw things the size I want so I'm going to draw myself really big, and I'll draw my big brother about half as big as I am."

Dad said, "Listen to this." Then he started to sing, "Row, row, row your boat, gently down the stream . . ."

We all joined in. We sang the song about ten times. Then Mom started singing, "She'll be comin' round the mountain when she comes . . ."

And we sang that song for a while. Then we sang "On top of old Smoky," "Someone's in the kitchen with Dinah," and some songs I had never sung before like "Don't sit under the apple tree with anyone else but me . . ."

We sang and sang until singing was no longer any fun. Then I had to go to the bathroom. "Already?" Dad said. "Didn't you go before we left?"

"Yes, I did, but I still have to go."

So we stopped at a gas station. Then we drove some more. I drew two more pictures, but I didn't show them to anyone. One of them was a picture of Gordey and our dog, Stubby. Stubby was way bigger than Gordey. Ha, ha.

We went down the highway a long time, and I watched a lot of telephone poles go by. I began to wonder how close we were to seeing the rabbits. Maybe we were almost there. The only way to find out was to ask. "Are we almost there?"

Dad said, "No, Dennis. We've only been on the road for about an hour and a half."

"Really? What time is it now?"

"It's about nine. We won't be there until long after we've eaten lunch."

We ate lunch on a bench at a rest stop. It was windy
and my glass of orange drink blew over. Also, when I was
eating my egg-salad sandwich, a big glop slid out and
landed on my shirt and pants. I tried to wipe it away, but
it just got messier and uglier.

"Dennis, Dennis," Mom said. "Let's see if I can clean that off." She got some wet paper towels and scrubbed the goop off, but she left a big wet stain. Gordey started laughing. Then mom laughed, too. When I looked at myself I laughed. I did look pretty bad.

To keep from going nuts during the rest of the trip, I thought about the rabbits we were going to see. I liked rabbits. Eddie once had a pet rabbit, and it was really big and neat. You could pet it and everything. I hoped we'd see some of those great big rabbits.

It felt like we had been driving for at least five hours, so I asked Dad, "How much longer before we get there?"

"Still a couple of hours," he said.

I waited a long, long time before I asked again. "Are we almost there yet?"

Mom said, "Don't ask those questions any more, Dennis. We'll be there when we get there."

Much, much later, we came to the edge of a large city. Dad turned around and said, "Well, folks, here we are. See the rabbits."

Everybody else said, "Yea."

I said, "Where are they?"

"Where are what?" Dad asked.

"The rabbits."

"What rabbits?"

"You said, 'see the rabbits.'"

Everybody was quiet for a little bit. Then Dad started to laugh. "Oh no," he said. "Not see the rabbits. Cedar Rapids. We're in Cedar Rapids, Iowa."

The others laughed. I didn't. I said, "Do you mean we're not going to see the rabbits? I thought that's why we were going here."

Gordey said, "You thought we were going to see rabbits? That's great. I can't wait to tell Eddie and the others. See the rabbits."

Ho, ho. Everybody else thought that was such a good joke. But I had really been looking forward to seeing those rabbits. And now . . . what a wasted trip.

When we finally got to Dick and Jen's place, they said
all those things that relatives say. "My, my, how you've
grown. Why, I never would have recognized Dennis.
He's quite a young man." Then I had to kiss them. I
didn't remember them at all, but they seemed nice.

They had fruit and nuts and other treats. I was eating
some of those curved nuts while everybody else went
into the kitchen. I could hear Dad telling them
something in the kind of voice he uses when he's trying
to keep a secret. Then everybody laughed. "See the
rabbits?" Dick shouted, and I had a pretty good idea
what Dad had told them. "That's amazing," Dick said.
"That boy must be a genius."

I got up and walked into the kitchen. I
wanted to know why I was
a genius. Both Dick and Jen looked very
surprised. Jen said, "Dennis seemed to know what
he was going to see."

"What do you mean?" Mom asked.

Jen said, "Just last week, Dick and I decided what
to do with the money we got from selling the store.
We decided to buy a rabbit ranch. We are now in the
business of raising pedigree rabbits. That's one of the
things we wanted you to see—all our beautiful rabbits."

"Wow," I said. "Do you have big ones?"

"We've got some of the very biggest rabbits you
have ever seen."

"This is amazing," Dad said. And he was right.

After supper, we went to the rabbit ranch, and we saw more rabbits than I had ever seen in my whole life. We saw spotted rabbits and black rabbits and white ones with pink eyes and white ones with blue eyes. We saw rabbits that were as big as our dog Stubby, and baby rabbits that were so small they could curl up in my hand. And we got to play with them. Were they ever a lot of fun.

And the next morning, Gordey and I got to go back there and feed them carrots and cabbage and clover. It was great. And that afternoon, when we were getting ready to go back home, guess what Dick and Jen gave us. I'll give you a hint. It was black and white, and it was in a big cage.

We didn't have a name for our rabbit at that time, but later we named her Clover because she really loves clover.

And when we got back home, I was the one who told the story about see-the-rabbits to Eddie and the others. I reminded Eddie, "Remember, I told you we were going to see the rabbits." Everybody thought I was pretty cool.

And when I got back to school, I drew one of my best pictures. It had me and Clover and Stubby and Gordey in it. And guess who was the smallest one in the whole picture. Gordey.

Why Leopard Has Black Spots

a story from the Dan people of Liberia

Told by Won-Ldy Paye
Edited by Margaret H. Lippert, Illustrated by Ted Eink

One day there was a spider. He was a great farmer. He lived in a village with a leopard and a deer. Spider had a BIG garden. He had so much food in his garden that every evening Spider would call Leopard and Deer and cook food for them.

But one day Spider went to his garden and noticed something was different. "Something is missing," he thought. Day after day things seemed to be missing.

At first he didn't care, because his garden was so big. But then it began to make him mad. One day he looked at his garden and said, "I saw a pumpkin here last night. Why is the pumpkin not here this morning?"

The next day he said, "I thought I saw a big cucumber here. Why is it not there?"

Spider began to check his farm very carefully. He was sure there were 98 tomatoes. But when he came back, there were 95. Man, this was really getting to Spider! He told his friends that his tomatoes were missing, but they laughed at him. "You want to tell me I'm not able to count right?" Spider asked.

Spider began to mark every single thing in his garden. Sometimes when he checked, instead of going from 1-2-3-4, the numbers went 1-3-5-7. And Spider said, "Something must be wrong!"

Spider went to Deer's hut. "Are you the one who is stealing from my garden all the time?"

Deer went: "Oh, no, no, no, no, no, no, no. Not me. You call for me every evening. You provide me dinner. Why should I go steal from your garden?"

Spider said, "I don't like stealing. I hope it's not you."

Deer said, "It's not me."

Spider went to Leopard. "Leopard, please be honest with me. Are you stealing from my garden?"

Leopard said, "No, I like meats. I really don't like too much veg-e-table. I am only eating veg-e-tables because you invite us to eat with you. You provide it for us."

Spider said, "Okay."

The vegetables kept on disappearing. Spider started to get really mad.

Spider went to Deer's house again. "Are you the one who's stealing from my garden?"

Deer said, "N-n-n-n-n-n-n-no!"

Spider said, "How come you're going 'n-n-no' like that?"

Deer said, "B-b-b-b-but that's the w-w-w-way I t-t-t-t-talk."

Spider said, "What! How come you don't talk like that all the time?"

Deer said, "When I'm m-m-m-m-mad, I t-t-t-t-talk like this." So Deer started pretending that he was mad, and that's why he was talking like this. Spider was really surprised because he never heard Deer talk like this before.

Then Spider went back to Leopard's House. "Are you the one who is stealing from my garden?"

Leopard said, "I told you I like meat. I don't like veg-e-table too much. So go ask Deer."

This time when Spider came to Deer, Deer said, "Here's what you should do: Go and dig a big hole in front of the entrance to the garden, and put a lot of fire in it and build it up. Cover it with a lot of dry branches. Let the fire burn way down. When the person who is stealing from your garden goes through the entrance, they'll fall in the fire. The next day when you come, you will see them."

So Spider went and dug the hole, and lit a fire in the bottom of it. He let the fire burn way down to red-hot coals, and then he covered the hole with dry branches, just as Deer said.

But Deer knew where the hole was, because Deer was the one who told Spider the trick. So Deer went around the hole and went into Spider's garden and stole other things. Then he ran to Leopard's house, and he said, "Spider called you."

Leopard said, "Where's Spider?'

Deer said, "Spider is in his garden."

So Leopard ran to the garden. When he went through the entrance to the garden, Leopard fell in the hole. And Leopard started to get burned.

Deer ran to Spider. Deer said, " Come! Come! Come! Come! I saw the person who is stealing from the garden all the time. We should keep this old Leopard down there fighting and trying to get up."

Spider shouted to Leopard: "You've been stealing from my garden all the time! Now I've got you."

Leopard said, "I don't know what you're talking about. I just want to get out of this fire."

Spider said, "Why have you been lying to me all the time? Every time you said you are not the one. Now my trap has caught you."

Leopard said, "I don't know what you're talking about. I just want to get out of this fire."

So Leopard leaped high. Ahhh, he got out of the fire. So Leopard said, "What is all this about?"

Spider said, "Deer told me I should play this trick. And now I find out who's been stealing."

And Leopard said, "But how come Deer came to me and said that you called me to the garden?"

Spider looked at Deer and said, "Did I send you to go get Leopard?"

The Deer said, "No."

Spider said, "Ohhhh, so it's you, Deer, who's been stealing from the garden all the time."

Leopard said, "WHAT! You did that! You did this to me? Because of your trick, I've got all these black spots on my skin because I got burned in the fire!"

Since that day, all the leopards we see have black, black, black spots all over their skin.

"You did this, Deer? Because of these black spots, anywhere I see you," Leopard said, "I'M GOING TO EAT YOU!" So Deer ran away. And Leopard ran after him.

Since that day, no matter how much you train the deer, no matter how much you train the leopard, don't put them together, because Leopard is sure going to eat Deer.

That's why Deer and Leopard aren't friends now, and that's why Leopard has black spots all over his skin.

Boar Out There

Written by Cynthia Rylant Illustrated by Fred Marvin

Everyone in Glen Morgan knew there was a wild boar in the woods over by the Miller farm. The boar was out beyond the splintery rail fence and past the old black Dodge that somehow had ended up in the woods and was missing most of its parts.

Jenny would hook her chin over the top rail of the fence, twirl a long green blade of grass in her teeth and whisper, "Boar out there."

And there were times she was sure she heard him. She imagined him running heavily through the trees, ignoring the sharp thorns and briars that raked his back and sprang away trembling.

She thought he might have a golden horn on his terrible head. The boar would run deep into the woods, then rise up on his rear hooves, throw his head toward the stars and cry a long, clear, sure note into the air. The note would glide through the night and spear the heart of the moon. The boar had no fear of the moon, Jenny knew, as she lay in bed, listening.

One hot summer day she went to find the boar. No one in Glen Morgan had ever gone past the old black Dodge and beyond, as far as she knew. But the boar was there somewhere, between those awful trees, and his dark green eyes waited for someone.

Jenny felt it was she.

Moving slowly over damp brown leaves, Jenny could sense her ears tingle and fan out as she listened for thick breathing from the trees. She stopped to pick a teaberry leaf to chew, stood a minute, then went on.

Deep in the woods she kept her eyes to the sky. She needed to be reminded that there was a world above and apart from the trees—a world of space and air, air that didn't linger all about her, didn't press deep into her skin, as forest air did.

Finally, leaning against a tree to rest, she heard him for the first time. She forgot to breathe, standing there listening to the stamping of hooves, and she choked and coughed.

Coughed!

And now the pounding was horrible, too
loud and confusing for Jenny. Horrible. She
stood stiff with wet eyes and knew she could
always pray, but for some reason didn't.

He came through the trees so fast that she
had no time to scream or run. And he was
there before her.

His large gray-black body shivered as he waited just beyond the shadow of the tree she held for support. His nostrils glistened, and his eyes; but astonishingly, he was silent. He shivered and glistened and was absolutely silent.

Jenny matched his silence, and her body was rigid, but not her eyes. They traveled along his scarred, bristling back to his thick hind legs. Tears spilling and flooding her face, Jenny stared at the boar's ragged ears, caked with blood. Her tears dropped to the leaves, and the only sound between them was his slow breathing.

Then the boar snorted and jerked. But Jenny did not move.

High in the trees a bluejay yelled, and, suddenly, it was over. Jenny stood like a rock as the boar wildly flung his head and in terror bolted past her.

Past her . . .

And now, since that summer, Jenny still hooks her chin over the old rail fence, and she still whispers, "Boar out there." But when she leans on the fence, looking into the trees, her eyes are full and she leaves wet patches on the splintery wood. She is sorry for the torn ears of the boar and sorry that he has no golden horn.

But mostly she is sorry that he lives in fear of bluejays and little girls, when everyone in Glen Morgan lives in fear of him.

Spaghetti

Written by Cynthia Rylant
Illustrated by Jim McGinnis

It was evening, and people sat outside, talking quietly among themselves. On the stoop of a tall building of crumbling bricks and rotting wood sat a boy. His name was Gabriel and he wished for some company.

Gabriel was thinking about things. He remembered being the only boy in class with the right answer that day, and he remembered the butter sandwich he had had for lunch. Gabriel was thinking that he would like to live outside all the time. He imagined himself carrying a pack of food and a few tools and a heavy cloth to erect a hasty tent. Gabriel saw himself sleeping among coyotes. But next he saw himself sleeping beneath the glittering lights of a movie theater, near the bus stop.

Gabriel was a boy who thought about things so seriously, so fully, that on this evening he nearly missed hearing a cry from the street. The cry was so weak and faraway in his mind that, for him, it could have been the slow lifting of a stubborn window. It could have been the creak of an old man's legs. It could have been the wind.

But it was not the wind, and it came to Gabriel slowly that he did, indeed, hear something, and that it did, indeed, sound like a cry from the street.

Gabriel picked himself up from the stoop and began to walk carefully along the edge of the street, peering into the gloom and the dusk. The cry came again and Gabriel's ears tingled and he walked faster.

He stared into the street, up and down it, knowing
something was there. The street was so gray that he
could not see . . . But not only the street was gray.

There, sitting on skinny stick-legs, wobbling to and
fro, was a tiny gray kitten. No cars had passed to
frighten it, and so it just sat in the street and cried its
windy, creaky cry and waited.

Gabriel was amazed. He had never imagined he
would be lucky enough one day to find a kitten. He
walked into the street and lifted the kitten into his hands.

Gabriel sat on the sidewalk with the kitten next to
his cheek and thought. The kitten smelled of pasta
noodles, and he wondered if it belonged to a friendly
Italian man somewhere in the city. Gabriel called the
kitten Spaghetti.

Gabriel and Spaghetti returned to the stoop. It occurred to Gabriel to walk the neighborhood and look for the Italian man, but the purring was so loud, so near his ear, that he could not think as seriously, as fully, as before.

Gabriel no longer wanted to live outside. He knew he had a room and a bed of his own in the tall building. So he stood up, with Spaghetti under his chin, and went inside to show his kitten where they would live together.

CHARLIE BEST

Written by Ruth Corrin
Illustrated by Lesley Moyes

On Monday, Charlie Best was late for school.

"What's the story?" said Ms. Noble. "Did you forget to get out of your bed?"

"No," said Charlie. "I did not forget to get out of my bed."

"Will you look at yourself?" said Ms. Noble. "What a mess. Your socks are all muddy. And, Charlie, your knees! Oh, just look at your pants!"

Charlie Best tucked in his shirt in, and thought about what to say. "Well, you see," he began, "it's like this . . .

160

I was tidy when I started out, and I was good and early, too. But on the way . . . I . . . bumped into a mountain. I really truly did! It was right in my way, and I had to climb over it."

"Oh, yes?" said Ms. Noble, "I don't see any mountains out there."

"It was a high mountain," said Charlie, "a steep mountain, an awfully slippery mountain, and there was snow on top!"

"Snow, was there?" said Ms. Noble.

"But I could only bring you a little bit," said Charlie. He could see she didn't believe him, so he scooped up a fresh lump of snow from the bottom of his schoolbag. "Snow," he said.

"Oh, Charlie," said Ms. Noble. She put the snow into an empty glass bowl on the nature table. "I see it, but I don't believe it!" she said.

"It took me such a long time to get to the top of that mountain," sighed Charlie. "That's what made me late. Luckily, it was quicker coming down. I slid down, see, on my bottom." And he bent over, and showed her the hole in his pants.

Ms. Noble did a quick bit of sewing. "No more mountains, please, Charlie," she said.

On Tuesday, the snow had melted into water, and Charlie Best was late again.

"What's the story?" said Ms. Noble. "Did you forget to get out of your bed?"

"No," said Charlie. "I did not forget to get out of my bed."

"Will you look at yourself?" said Ms. Noble. "What a mess! You're all wet, Charlie, and it isn't even raining! Oh, just look at your clothes!"

Charlie Best buttoned his shirt, and thought about what to say. "Well, you see," he began, "it's like this . . .

I was tidy when I started out, and I was good and early, too. But on the way . . . I . . . tripped into a river. I really truly did! It was right in my way, so I had to wade all the way across."

"Oh, yes?" said Ms. Noble. "I don't see any rivers out there."

"It was a green river," said Charlie, "a cold river, a wonderfully wide river, and there were twelve little red fishes swimming in it."

"Fishes, were there?" said Ms. Noble.

"But I could only bring you one," said Charlie. He could see she didn't believe him, so he reached into his rubber boot and pulled out a wriggly red fish by its tail. "Fishes," he said.

"Oh, Charlie," said Ms. Noble. She put the fish into the glass bowl with the water that used to be snow. "I see it, but I don't believe it," she said.

"It took me such a long time to get to the other side of that river," sighed Charlie. "That's what made me late. Luckily, I had my rubber boots on. Good things, rubber boots. See?"

And he emptied both his rubber boots out, right there, on the floor.

Ms. Noble handed Charlie a mop. "No more rivers, please, Charlie," she said.

On Wednesday, the fish was still swimming in the water that used to be snow, and there was Charlie Best, late again.

"What's the story?" said Ms. Noble. "Did you forget to get out of your bed?"

"No," said Charlie. "I did not forget to get out of my bed."

"Will you look at yourself?" said Ms. Noble. "What a mess! There's a bird's nest on your head. And, Charlie, your face! Oh, just look at your hair!"

Charlie Best pulled his socks up, and thought about what to say. "Well, you see," he began, "it's like this . . .

I was tidy when I started out, and I was good and early, too. But on the way . . . I . . . walked into a forest. I really truly did! It was right in my way, so I had to tramp right through it."

"Oh, yes?" said Ms. Noble. "I don't see any forests out there."

"It was a deep forest," said Charlie, "a thick forest, a particularly prickly forest, and there were twenty-nine spotted birds hiding in it."

171

"Birds, were there?" said Ms. Noble.

"But I could only bring you one," said Charlie. He could see she didn't believe him, so he gave a long, loud whistle, and a beautiful spotted bird flew into the room. "Birds," he said.

"Oh, Charlie," said Ms. Noble. She tried, but couldn't catch it. "I see it, but I don't believe it," she said.

"It took me such a long time to learn how to whistle like that," sighed Charlie. "That's what made me late. Luckily, I brought her nest along. It's got something in it. See?" Then Charlie Best untangled the nest from his hair. There were three spotted eggs in it.

Ms. Noble made a space for the nest on the nature table beside the fish, and the water that used to be snow. "No more forests, please, Charlie," she said.

On Thursday, the spotted bird was sitting on the eggs in her nest. And there was Charlie Best, late again.

"What's the story?" said Ms. Noble. "Did you forget to get out of your bed?"

"No," said Charlie. "I did not forget to get out of my bed."

"Will you look at yourself?" said Ms. Noble. "What a mess! You're all tangled with rope. You've lost one of your shoes. Oh, just look at your shirt!"

Charlie hitched his pants up, and thought about what to say. "Well, you see," he began, "it's like this . . .

I was tidy when I started out, and I was good and early, too. But on the way . . . I . . . fell into a cave. I really truly did! It was right in my way, so I had to be very brave and grope my way through it."

"Oh, yes?" said Ms. Noble. "I don't see any caves out there."

"It was a huge cave," said Charlie, "a damp cave, a dreadfully dark cave, and there were thirty-two dragons roaring in it!"

"Dragons, were there?" said Ms. Noble.

"But I could only bring you one," said Charlie, though he could see she didn't believe him.

"I don't see any dragon," said Ms. Noble, and winked at the other children. "Is it in your schoolbag?"

"It was a yellow dragon," said Charlie, "a bellowing dragon, and it licked me all over."

"Yellow, was it?" Ms. Noble looked under Charlie's hat. "I don't see any dragon," she said.

"It was a rumbly dragon," said Charlie, "a loud dragon, a horribly hot dragon, and it breathed green steam."

"Breathed steam, did it?" said Ms. Noble. "I don't see any dragon. Is it in your pocket?"

The other children were jumping up and down. Ms. Noble held her sides and laughed and laughed, the spotted bird whistled, and the wriggly fish swam round and round and round in the water that used to be snow.

"It took me such a long time to get out of that cave," said Charlie.

Ms. Noble's sides were sore from so much laughing. "Well, it would," she said, "especially with a dragon! I suppose that's what made you late."

"Right," said Charlie. "Luckily, I had this rope with me. You need a rope when you've got a dragon to catch. Don't you agree?"

Then Charlie Best took hold of his tangled rope, and pulled.

The other children stopped jumping up and down.
Ms. Noble stopped laughing, and took two steps backward.
The spotted bird stopped whistling, and the wriggly red fish
stopped swimming round and round in the water that used
to be snow.

"Oh, Charlie," whispered Ms. Noble.
"I see, but I don't believe it!"
Then everyone was quiet.

Tied to the other end of Charlie Best's rope was a rumbly, yellow dragon!

Ms. Noble sat down. "No more caves, please, Charlie," she said.

On Friday, the spotted bird was still there on her nest, and the fish was still swimming in the water that used to be snow. And Charlie Best was the first kid at school. He had his dragon with him.

"I see it, but I don't believe it," said Ms. Noble. She wasn't looking at the dragon; she was looking at Charlie. "Will you look at yourself?" she said. "You're tidy!"

Charlie looked down at his clothes. Even his shirt was tucked in.

"What's the story, Charlie Best? Couldn't you find any caves today? No rivers to wade? No forests to tramp? Not even a mountain to climb?"

The dragon yawned a yellow yawn, and let out a cloud of green steam. Ms. Noble opened the window.

Charlie was embarrassed. "Well, you see," he began, "it's like this . . .

I was tidy when I started out, and I was good and early, too . . ."

"That's what I like to see, Charlie," said Ms. Noble, and the dragon gave him a hot, yellow lick.

"But I didn't want to be early," said Charlie, "and I tried to get my clothes messed up, I really truly did. All I needed was a cave, or a river to cross, or a forest, or even a mountain to climb. I wanted to do all those things. But . . . and it's not fair . . .

my dragon wouldn't let me!"

Steps

by Deborah M. Newton Chocolate

Illustrated by Morissa Lipstein

"Somebody has to take the first step," said Sonny and Jamal's mother.

"Your Mama's right," said their father. But the two nine-year-old boys sat quietly, staring at each other. They were new stepbrothers.

"Okay, boys," said their father. "Your mother and I still have boxes to unpack. So while we're doing that, why don't you two spend some time getting to know each other better."

"But, Dad," groaned Jamal, jumping up from his bed, "I have baseball practice."

"Mama?" whined Sonny.

"Family is a lot more important than baseball," said their mother, as both parents left the room.

When the door was closed, Jamal threw himself on the bed. "I wish you would've never come here to live!" he said.

"I wish I didn't live here, either," Sonny shot back at him. He looked around and quickly decided that Jamal's room wasn't big enough for the two of them to share.

"Well, that's one thing we both agree on," said Jamal.

"What's that?" Sonny said.

"We both wish you'd never have come here!"

Later that evening, Jamal's father began unpacking a big sewing machine from a heavy wooden crate.

"Look!" said Sonny, pointing to a leg on the sewing machine. "That leg is loose. One of the screws must have fallen out again."

Jamal and his father knelt down beside the sewing machine and looked underneath. "You're right," said their father. "But how did you know a screw was missing?"

"That screw was always falling out at Grandma's house," explained Sonny. "Every time Grandma got in the mood to clean, Grandpa and I had to move this old machine from room to room. And that screw was always falling out."

"Well, if the machine is that old," cracked Jamal, "why don't you just throw it out and buy a new one?"

Sonny took a deep breath. He could feel his ears turning hot, the way they always did when he was angry.

Their father put his hands on Sonny's shoulders. "Take it easy, son," he said. And then he turned to Jamal.

"Listen to me, Jamal," said their father. "Sonny is your stepbrother. And while this sewing machine may seem old to you, it means a lot to Sonny."

Jamal didn't say anything, but he didn't like the way his father was taking Sonny's side.

"In the morning," their dad said, "I want you both to go to the hardware store. We'll buy some screws and fix up this sewing machine like new for your mother."

"Aw, no!" complained Jamal. "First no baseball, and now this!"

Later, in bed that night, Jamal couldn't help thinking about how his father had stood up for Sonny. Sonny was putting his pajamas on now. When he finished, he crossed the room and opened the window.

"What do you think you're doing?" Jamal asked.

"What does it look like I'm doing?" Sonny said. "I'm opening the window."

"Let's get one thing straight," said Jamal, getting up from his bed. "This is my side of the room. And, this is my hockey stick," he said, picking up his stick. "And, this is my baseball mitt. Get it?"

Sonny just looked at Jamal. Then, he climbed into bed and turned his back on his stepbrother.

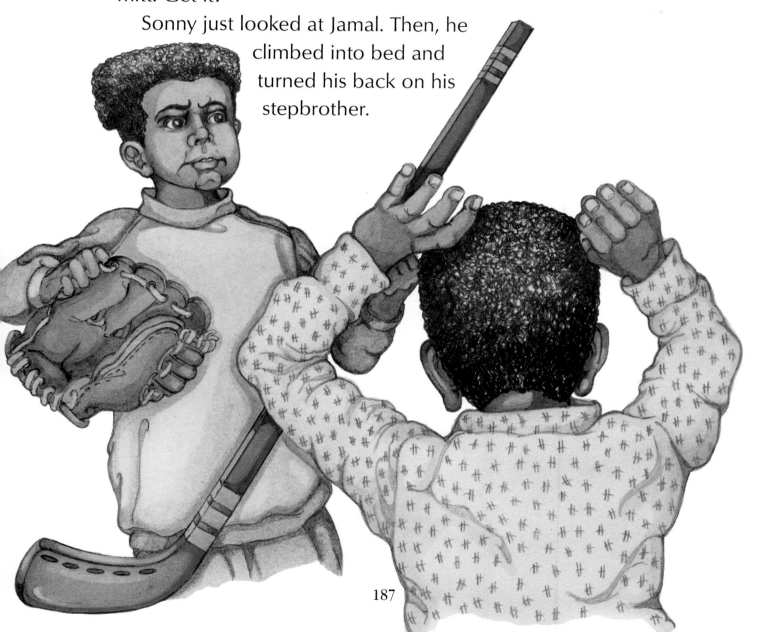

The next day, after breakfast, the two boys grabbed their bicycles and started out for the hardware store. Jamal knew the neighborhood better, so he sped through the streets. It was hard for Sonny to keep up with him. And, to make matters worse, Jamal kept confusing Sonny by darting in and out of narrow side streets.

Before long, they came to a vacant lot where Jamal stopped to catch his breath. The lot was covered with huge sand hills.

With a mean smile on his face, Jamal said to Sonny, "Let's ride some hills."

"I don't think we should," said Sonny.

"You're not chicken, are you," Jamal asked. He began to tease Sonny. "Here chick, chick, chick, chick, chick!" he said. Sonny could feel his ears turning hot again.

"Come on, Sonny!" Jamal dared. "One ride won't hurt."

Sonny didn't want Jamal to know that he had broken his arm once, riding on a dirt hill.

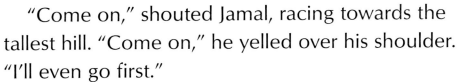

"Come on," shouted Jamal, racing towards the tallest hill. "Come on," he yelled over his shoulder. "I'll even go first."

Before Sonny could say anything, Jamal had reached the hill and was already climbing fast.

Suddenly Sonny saw Jamal flying head first down a steep bank of the hill. Without thinking, Sonny pedaled as hard as he could until he reached the bottom of the hill where his stepbrother lay.

"Owwwww!" moaned Jamal. "My leg!" he cried. "I think it's broken."

Sonny leaped off his bike. He tried to help Jamal get on his feet.

"Get up," pleaded Sonny.

Jamal's leg hurt so badly, he felt like crying. But he wouldn't cry—not in front of Sonny.

"Never mind. Don't move anymore," said Sonny. "I don't want to leave you here alone, but I have to go get help."

Both boys became quiet. Sonny quickly scanned the area around the vacant lot. There was a small grocery store on the corner. He could get help there.

Jamal began to look scared, and Sonny knew that his leg must really hurt. Sonny knelt down beside Jamal and looked straight into his eyes. When he spoke, his voice was a lot calmer than he felt.

"I'm going to the store to get help. Just rest on the ground and don't move. I'll be back as soon as I can."

Jamal didn't say anything, but he lay back obediently and prepared to wait. Sonny got on his bike and sped off toward the store.

The next hour was kind of a blur to Sonny. Two phone calls from the grocery store brought their parents and an Emergency Squad to the vacant lot. The next thing Sonny knew, they were all on their way to a hospital.

At the hospital, the doctor told them, "That broken leg means no more baseball this summer."

Sonny sat at his stepbrother's bedside and saw the disappointment in his face.

Suddenly, Sonny heard himself saying, "I'll help you keep your pitching arm in shape." And then he smiled and said, "For that you won't need legs."

Jamal looked at Sonny. And, for the first time, he felt sure that they could be not only stepbrothers, but friends.

"You know?" said Jamal. "For a stepbrother, you're not half bad!"

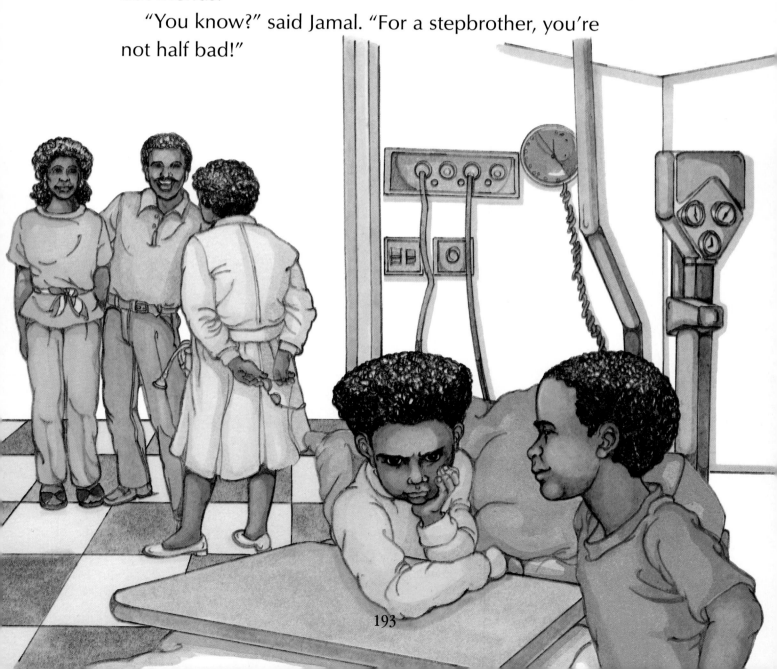

The next afternoon, Sonny and Jamal were sitting on the front porch. They heard someone calling Jamal's name.

"Hey, Jamal!" came a voice from across the yard. It was his next-door neighbor Rudy, who had been away on vacation all summer.

"I heard about your leg," Rudy said. "That's a swell cast," he said when he came closer. "May I sign it?"

"Sure," said Jamal, handing him some colored markers.

"Hi!" said Rudy to Sonny, noticing him for the very first time.

"Hi!" said Sonny.

"Is he your cousin, Jamal?" Rudy asked. Rudy was bent over Jamal's cast, writing his name in bright neon colors. Jamal and Sonny looked at each other and laughed.

"Naw," answered Jamal. "He's not my cousin." Smiling, Jamal said proudly, "Rudy, meet Sonny—my new step!"

The Soup Stone

A Belgian folk tale retold by Maria Leach
Illustrated by Karen Bauman

One day a soldier was walking home from the wars and came to a village. The wind was cold; the sky was gray, and the soldier was hungry. He stopped at a house on the edge of the village and asked for something to eat. "We have nothing for ourselves," the people said, so the soldier went on.

He stopped at the next house and asked for something to eat. "We have nothing for ourselves," the people said.

"Have you got a big pot?" the soldier asked. Yes, they had a big iron pot.

"Have you got water?" he asked. Yes, they had plenty of water.

"Fill the pot with water and put it on the fire," the soldier said, "for I have a soup stone with me."

"A soup stone?" they asked. "What is that?"

"It is a stone that makes soup," the soldier replied. And they all gathered round to see this wonder.

The woman of the house filled the big pot with water and hung it over the fire. The soldier took a stone from his pocket (it looked like any stone a man might pick up on the road) and tossed it into the pot. "Now let it boil," he said. So they all sat down to wait for the pot to boil.

"Could you spare a bit of salt for it?" the soldier asked.

"Of course," the woman said, and she pulled out the salt box. The soldier took a fistful of salt and threw it in, for it was a big pot. Then they all sat back to wait.

"A few carrots would taste good in it," the soldier said longingly.

"Oh, we have a few carrots," the woman said, and she pulled them out from under a bench, where the soldier had been eyeing them. So they threw in the carrots. And while the carrots boiled, the soldier told them stories of his adventures.

"A few potatoes would be good, wouldn't they?" the soldier said. "They'd thicken the soup a bit."

"We have a few potatoes," said the oldest girl. "I'll get them." So they put the potatoes in the pot and waited for the soup to boil.

"An onion does give a good flavor," the soldier said.

"Run next door and ask the neighbor for an onion," the farmer told his smallest son. The child ran out of the house and came back with three onions. So they put the onions in. While they were waiting, they were cracking jokes and telling tales.

". . . And I haven't tasted cabbage since I left my mother's house," the soldier was saying.

"Run out into the garden and pull a cabbage," said the mother. And a small girl ran out and came back with a cabbage. And they put that in.

"It won't be long now," the soldier said.

"Just a little longer," the woman said, stirring the pot with a long ladle.

199

At that moment the oldest son came in. He had
been hunting and brought home two rabbits.

"Just what we need for the finishing touch!" cried
the soldier, and it was only a matter of minutes before
the rabbits were cut up and thrown into the pot.

"Ha!" said the hungry hunter. "The smell of a
fine soup."

"The traveler has brought a soup stone," the farmer
said to his son, "and he is making soup with it in the pot."

At last the soup was ready, and it was good. There was enough for all: the soldier and the farmer and his wife, the oldest girl and the oldest son, the little girl, and the little son.

"It's a wonderful soup," the farmer said.

"It's a wonderful stone," the wife said.

"It is," the soldier said, "and it will make soup forever if you follow the formula we used today."

So they finished the soup. And when the soldier said good-bye, he gave the woman the stone to pay back the kindness. She protested politely.

"It's nothing," the soldier said and went on his way without the stone.

Luckily, he found another just before he came to the next village.

Amelia Bedelia

by Peggy Parish
Pictures by Fritz Siebel

"Oh, Amelia Bedelia, your first day of work, and I can't be here. But I made a list for you. You do just what the list says," said Mrs. Rogers.

Mrs. Rogers got into the car with Mr. Rogers. They drove away.

"My, what nice folks. I'm going to like working here," said Amelia Bedelia.

Amelia Bedelia went inside. "Such a grand house. These must be rich folks. But I must get to work. Here I stand just looking. And me with a whole list of things to do."

Amelia Bedelia stood there a minute longer.

"I think I'll make a surprise for them. I'll make lemon-meringue pie. I do make good pies."

So Amelia Bedelia went into the kitchen. She put a little of this and a pinch of that into a bowl. She mixed and she rolled.

Soon her pie was ready to go into the oven.
"There," said Amelia Bedelia. "That's done."

"Now let's see what this list says."
Amelia Bedelia read,

Change the towels in the green bathroom.

Amelia Bedelia found the green bathroom.
"Those towels are very nice. Why change them?"
she thought.

Then Amelia Bedelia remembered what Mrs. Rogers had said. She must do just what the list told her.

"Well, all right," said Amelia Bedelia. Amelia Bedelia got some scissors. She snipped a little here and a little there. And she changed those towels.

"There," said Amelia Bedelia. She looked at her list again.

Dust the furniture.

"Did you ever hear tell of such a silly thing. At my house we undust the furniture. But to each his own way."

Amelia Bedelia took one last look at
the bathroom. She saw a big box with
the words *Dusting Powder* on it.

"Well, look at that. A special powder to dust with!" exclaimed Amelia Bedelia. So Amelia Bedelia dusted the furniture.

"That should be dusty enough. My, how nice it smells."

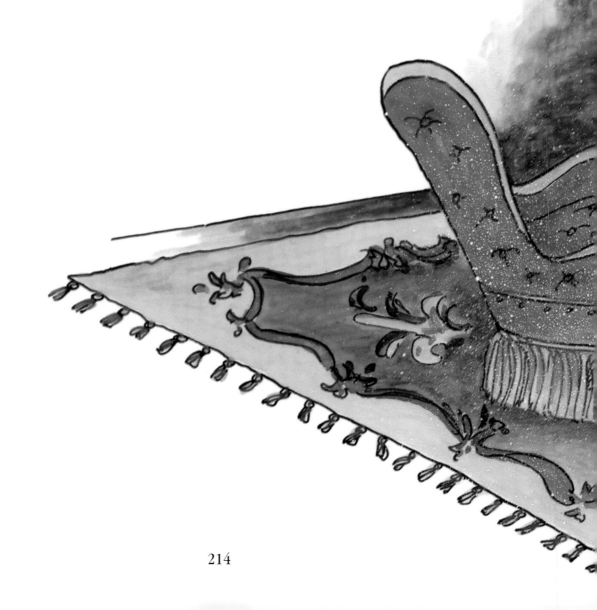

Draw the drapes when the sun comes in.

read Amelia Bedelia. She looked up. The sun was coming in. Amelia Bedelia looked at the list again.

"Draw the drapes? That's what it says. I'm not much of a hand at drawing, but I'll try."

So Amelia Bedelia sat right down and
she drew those drapes.

Amelia Bedelia marked off about the drapes.
"Now what?"

Put the lights out when you finish in the living room.

Amelia Bedelia thought about this a minute.
She switched off the lights. Then she carefully
unscrewed each bulb.

And Amelia Bedelia put the lights out. "So those things need to be aired out, too. Just like pillows and babies. Oh, I do have a lot to learn."

"My pie!" exclaimed Amelia Bedelia.
She hurried to the kitchen.

"Just right," she said. She took the pie
out of the oven and put it on the table to
cool. Then she looked at the list.

Measure two cups of rice.

"That's next," said Amelia Bedelia.

Amelia Bedelia found two cups. She filled them with rice.

And Amelia Bedelia measured that rice.

Amelia Bedelia laughed.

"These folks do want me to do funny things."

Then she poured the rice back into the container.

The meat market will deliver a steak and a chcken.

Please trim the fat before you put the steak in the icebox.

And please dress the chicken.

When the meat arrived, Amelia Bedelia
opened the bag. She looked at the steak for
a long time.

"Yes," she said. "That will do nicely."

Amelia Bedelia got some lace and bits of ribbon. And Amelia Bedelia trimmed that fat before she put the steak in the icebox.

"Now I must dress the chicken. I wonder if she wants a he chicken or a she chicken?" said Amelia Bedelia. Amelia Bedelia went right to work. Soon the chicken was finished.

Amelia Bedelia heard the door open.
"The folks are back," she said. She rushed
out to meet them.

"Amelia Bedelia, why are all the light bulbs outside?" asked Mr. Rogers.

"The list just said to put the lights
out," said Amelia Bedelia. "It didn't say to
bring them back in. Oh, I do hope they
didn't get aired too long."

"Amelia Bedelia, the sun will fade the furniture. I asked you to draw the drapes," said Mrs. Rogers.

"I did! I did! See," said Amelia Bedelia.

She held up her picture.

Then Mrs. Rogers saw the furniture.
"The furniture!" she cried.

"Did I dust it well enough?"
asked Amelia Bedelia. "That's such
nice dusting powder."

Mr. Rogers went to wash his hands.
"I say," he called. "These are very
unusual towels."

Mrs. Rogers dashed into the bathroom.
"Oh, my best towels," she said.
"Didn't I change them enough?"
asked Amelia Bedelia.

Mrs. Rogers went to the kitchen.
"I'll cook the dinner. Where is the
rice I asked you to measure?"

"I put it back in the container. But I
remember—it measured four and a half inches,"
said Amelia Bedelia.

"Was the meat delivered?" asked Mrs. Rogers.

"Yes," said Amelia Bedelia. "I trimmed the fat just like you said. It does look nice."

Mrs. Rogers rushed to the icebox. She opened it.

"Lace! Ribbons! Oh, dear!" said Mrs. Rogers.

"The chicken—you dressed the chicken?" asked Mrs. Rogers.

"Yes, and I found the nicest box to put him in," said Amelia Bedelia.

"Box!" exclaimed Mrs. Rogers. Mrs. Rogers hurried over to the box. She lifted the lid. There lay the chicken. And he was just as dressed as he could be.

Mrs. Rogers was angry. She was very angry. She opened her mouth. Mrs. Rogers meant to tell Amelia Bedelia she was fired. But before she could get the words out, Mr. Rogers put something in her mouth. It was so good Mrs. Rogers forgot about being angry.

"Lemon-meringue pie!" she exclaimed.

"I made it to surprise you," said Amelia Bedelia happily.

So right then and there Mr. and Mrs. Rogers decided that Amelia Bedelia must stay. And so she did. Mrs. Rogers learned to say undust the furniture, unlight the lights, close the drapes, and things like that.

Mr. Rogers didn't care if Amelia Bedelia trimmed all his steaks with lace.

All he cared about was having her there to make lemon-meringue pie.

My (Wow!) Summer VACATION

by Susan Cornell Poskanzer
Illustrated by Meryl Henderson

I'd heard about the rattlesnakes. I'd heard about the scorpions. I'd heard about the red fire ants whose bites make your skin think it's in flames. So when Mom asked me, "How'd you like to raft down the Colorado River for eight days through the Grand Canyon in Arizona?" you can imagine what I said.

"What's wrong with staying in New Jersey?" I answered. "My friends are here. And there are no rattlesnakes, scorpions, or fire ants."

"Don't be silly," Mom said. "You'll have a great time."

That's how I found myself in the middle of the huge rocky cliffs called the Grand Canyon.

I was the only kid on our raft, a rubber contraption with a motor, giant pontoons, four big supply boxes, and 16 people. Our guides, Owen and P.J., were comforting from the start of the trip at Lee's Ferry.

"We shouldn't see more than a dozen or so rattlesnakes," joked Owen.

"It's the height of lizard season, especially gila monsters," said P.J. flashing me a smile.

I pretended to ignore him. I didn't think much of this trip from the start. In fact, I had just three little goals. I wrote them on the back of our guidebook.

The guidebook had a map of the river showing what we might see at each mile. I flipped through the book, looking for rattlesnakes. I found the names of 14 other snakes I hadn't even heard of. I was figuring out which ones sounded poisonous, when Mom shouted, "Put the book down, and listen to how to live through the rapids." Remembering Goal Number Three, I put away the book and listened.

"The river can be dangerous," began Owen, "especially the rapids. And we'll meet some of the biggest in the world. Just wait until you see Lava Falls!" His eyes lit up. "It's a whopper!"

"Never take off your life jacket in the raft . . . even when we're not in the rapids," warned P.J.

They showed us how to squeeze onto the floor of the raft like fancy sardines and hold on to the side ropes. I looked at the names in black letters on our day-glow orange life jackets. They sounded silly . . . Red Hawk, Honeybunch, Nankoweap, Foo Foo, and Havasu to name a few. I was Foo Foo. . .and not too happy about it. But these names could instantly show who needed help or who was missing.

I looked around and suddenly felt very small. The cliffs, which had been quite low when we launched the raft, were slowly inching up. Rising layers of sand-colored rock grew on both sides of the river. The river itself was green and cold. It was so cold it chilled the bags of drinks the raft dragged along behind it. We also dragged bags for garbage. Sixteen thousand people lived on the river, camping on the sandy beaches each year. And they all carried out the garbage they made. We wouldn't even build campfires at night because as P.J. said, "The canyon is so special. We don't want to scar it."

Did I mention that it was hot? Well, it was . . . at least 100 degrees. As I splashed myself with icy river water, I suddenly saw two huge sheep staring at me from the shore. They were very still. Big horns curled out of their heads and looked as if they were listening with giant ears. And then, suddenly, they ran away. . .straight up a ragged cliff.

Just then I heard Owen holler, "Get ready for Badger Creek Rapid!"

We sat down, criss-crossing the raft and holding on to the ropes, just as we'd been taught.

Suddenly, the river foamed as we turned around and slid through the rapid backward! The rushing water swirled, lurched, and rose around us, playing with the big raft as if it were a tiny mouse. Mom looked scared. Dad looked even more scared. I laughed out loud. This was fun! I couldn't wait to see Lava Falls Rapid now. This trip might work out to be all right after all! Then I touched my head. It was bare. My lucky hat was gone . . . lost to the rapid forever! Goal Number Two was doomed.

That night I moped around the camp. I paid no attention to the mule deer that appeared on the North Rim of the canyon during dinner. I hardly looked at the bats fluttering around at dusk. I barely noticed the wicked-looking blood-red rocks that seemed to sneak closer when we weren't looking. I just thought about my lucky baseball hat.

"It may turn up, Foo Foo," said Dad.

All night I worried about going down the river without my hat. In the morning I was surprised to wake up in the canyon.

That was easy, considering what happened later that day. We'd drifted down the river with the motor off. It was so silent, so peaceful. Then suddenly, Owen steered over to a small beach.

"Everybody out of the raft," he ordered. "Go see the cavern on the far side of this beach," he said calmly. "Look in the rocks. You'll find some special things."

He was right. The rocks were carved with deep fossils that looked like sea squids. It was hard to believe, but once there was an ocean here. Then later, the river took billions of years to carve its slow, steady way through the rock to form this amazing canyon.

When we returned to the raft, I smugly checked off Goal Number One. Owen was smiling a sly smile.

"What's up?" I asked him.

He couldn't wait to tell me.

"When we were drifting along back there, I suddenly saw a rattlesnake's head pop up right next to Foo-Foo," he laughed.

I gasped so hard, I hiccupped.

"So I shooed you all out of the raft and over to the cavern. Then I flipped the snake over with the emergency oar. . . right onto the beach. He's there . . . under that brittlebush."

He pointed to a rattler with inky black diamonds printed along a fat, muscular body. Its pale eyes looked up at me like a ghostly mask. But the snake seemed tired and sad, coiled up in the shade. It looked beautiful, too. I wished it would rattle. I even wished I could touch it. From then on, I kept my eyes open for other rattlers. I wondered if they were all so beautiful. I never did find another one, but I saw other things.

Sometimes hikers lined high canyon ledges, like fire ants heading home.

Once a shimmering emerald-green hummingbird hovered over the raft, eating bits of sweet plum from my hand.

Another time, P.J. let me use our net to pluck things from the river. We found something almost every day. One day we fished up three juice cans, a water bottle, and a pair of baggy pants. We added them to our garbage bags to take out of the canyon.

One morning we drifted to a super-ugly black rock sticking right up in the middle of the river.

"Before each trip through Lava Falls, the youngest on board must kiss Vulcan's Anvil for good luck," announced Owen.

Everyone looked at me. I looked at Vulcan's Anvil and knew I didn't want to kiss it. But before I could complain, Owen had picked me up over the side of the raft. So I gave that gross rock a quick kiss and everyone cheered. Well after all, I didn't want to jinx our run through Lava! I wiped my mouth on my shirt about three times.

Suddenly, we knew we were nearing something enormous. We could hear it. We could feel it. Finally, we saw it. Lava Falls lay just ahead. Owen and P.J. stopped to plan their attack on the great rush of water. They studied the rapid, talking quietly. Finally, they both pointed thumbs up, and we all got back into the raft. Then we started toward the rapid.

I was sure everyone could hear my heart beat as the water swirled around us. We rode the rapid backward, as we did others. But this one was different. The engine rumbled, working hard to fight the great rush. Water crashed like thunder. Deep whirls sucked old trees and branches under. Water foamed and turned brown as it scraped dirt and rocks up from the bottom. The river flowed into the raft, drenching us all. We screamed with each bump on this roller coaster of water.

Just when it seemed the raft would flip over, and we'd all be sucked under the rocks and trees, Lava Falls Rapid was behind us. Everyone whooped and cheered.

Then suddenly, I saw it . . . a patch of blue in the water.

"Get the net," I yelled, but P.J. already had it. In a flash, he scooped up my lost lucky hat and flipped it onto my head. The hat had floated down the river with us! Cold water trickled out of the hat and onto my face.

"Miracles like this happen all the time in the canyon," said Owen patting my shoulder.

My mom was right all along. I was one of the lucky ones. Now I didn't want to leave the canyon. Who cared about New Jersey!

But the next afternoon, our time was up. As we walked out of the Grand Canyon at Diamond Creek, I checked off Goals Two and Three. Then I printed one more goal in giant letters.

MY GOALS FOR THIS TRIP
✓ 1. See some neat fossils.
✓ 2. Hang on to my lucky baseball hat.
3. Come home alive.

4. Come back and visit the Grand Canyon again.